Do You Want to Be a
Roman Soldier?

Written by
Fiona Macdonald

Illustrated by
Nicholas Hewetson

BOOK HOUSE

This edition first published in MMXV by Book House

Distributed by Black Rabbit Books
P.O. Box 3263
Mankato
Minnesota MN 56002

Cataloging-in-Publication Data is available
from the Library of Congress

ISBN: 978-1-909645-38-7

Series created and designed by David Salariya
Penny Clarke, Consultant Editor
Karen Barker Smith, Editor

Stephen Johnson, Fact Consultant
Director of Operations, Heritage Lottery Fund, and author of several books on Roman archaeology

Photographic credits
t=top b=bottom c=center l=left r=right

The Art Archive / Archaeological Museum
Châtillon-sur-Seine / Dagli Orti: 23
The Art Archive / Archaeological Museum
Venice / Dagli Orti (A): 13, 28t
The Art Archive / Dagli Orti: 27t
The Art Archive / Musée du Louvre Paris / Dagli
Orti: 28b

The Art Archive / Museo Nazionale Terme Rome / Dagli
Orti: 7, 27c
Doug Smith: 10, 17
Every effort has been made to trace copyright holders. The Salariya
Book Company apologizes for any unintentional omissions and
would be pleased, in such cases, to add an acknowledgment in
future editions.

Soldiers Needed

Ⓗow would you like to join the Roman army?

Roman legions are based throughout the Roman Empire. There are vacancies for young men who want to spread the Pax Romana (Roman peace). You will bring the benefits of Roman civilization to barbarians and enjoy an interesting, well-paid career. Foot soldiers and cavalrymen are needed.

Your main duties will include:

- defending the city of Rome, its empire, and its frontiers from enemy attack

- marching to put down rebellions in conquered lands

- digging ramparts and ditches, building forts, and constructing roads

- obeying orders and fighting bravely as part of a team

Apply to the army headquarters in your provincial capital for a medical checkup and an interview.

Contents

What Applicants Should Know

Be prepared for a journey back in time almost two thousand years. You're going to the mighty Roman Empire at the height of its power, around A.D. 130. The map below shows the Roman Empire at its greatest extent—an enormous territory stretching from southern Scotland to the Caspian Sea. All conquered lands send goods and money to Rome as tribute and taxes. In return, Roman soldiers and government officials are stationed all around the empire to see that it is well defended and properly run. Many local leaders are happy to work with Roman rulers. Others are hostile. One resentful British chieftain has complained, "What the Romans call empire-building is just plundering, butchering, and theft!"

The Roman Empire

Second century A.D.

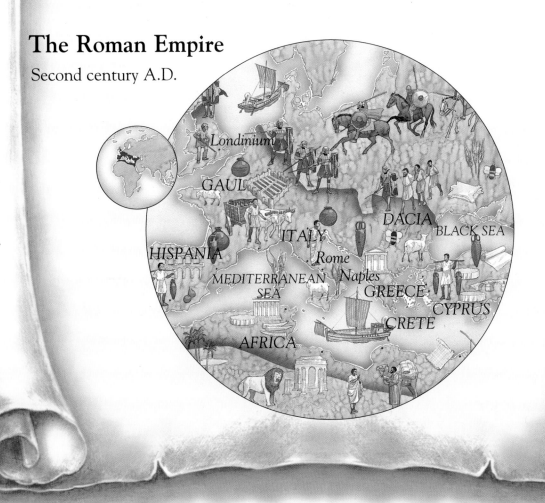

Londinium

GAUL

HISPANIA

ITALY

Rome

Naples

MEDITERRANEAN SEA

DACIA

BLACK SEA

GREECE

CYPRUS

CRETE

AFRICA

Comrades in Arms

To join the army, you must be young, male, slim, healthy, and at least five feet, nine inches (1.75 m) tall. You need good eyesight and hearing and the ability to speak Latin. If you are a Roman citizen, born in the Roman Empire, you are just the man we need. Even if you are not a Roman citizen you can still enroll, as long as you are not a slave.

How a legion is divided

▼ There are about 300,000 soldiers in the entire Roman army, and the elite troops (120,000 men) are divided into 25 legions.

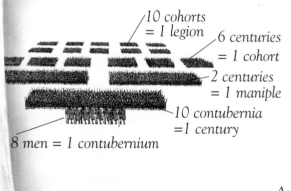

10 cohorts = 1 legion

6 centuries = 1 cohort

2 centuries = 1 maniple

10 contubernia = 1 century

8 men = 1 contubernium

Standard-bearers

▼ These soldiers are standard-bearers (*signiferi*). Chosen for their bravery, they carry their legion's standard (an emblem) in battle. They also look   after the soldiers' pay and savings.

We walk 24 miles (39 km) each day, defending the frontier for Rome.

Baggage wagon

Auxiliary archers

Auxiliary officers

Standard-bearer

Auxiliary centurions

The sign of Rome

▼ The letters SPQR stand for Senatus Populusque Romanus. It means "the Senate and people of Rome."

Aquila (eagle)

SPQR

Legionary soldiers

Legionary centurion

Legionary or auxiliary?

There are two different types of soldier in the Roman army—legionaries and auxiliaries. If you're a Roman citizen you can join as a legionary. If you're not a Roman citizen, you'll be recruited as an auxiliary. You will provide extra manpower to assist the legionaries. You could also be deployed as an expert to fight using your own native techniques.

Battle scene carved in marble

Soldiers in stone

▲ This carving on a decorative coffin shows Roman soldiers fighting against the Dacians in present-day eastern Europe.

Army on the march

▼ Where would you fit into this army? The commander rides in front, followed by bodyguards, musicians, and standard-bearers. Then comes a legionary centurion with a century of legionaries (regular soldiers), two auxiliary centurions on horseback, their standard-bearer, two auxiliary cavalry officers, auxiliary archers, and finally the baggage wagon.

Standard-bearers

Musicians

Legionary bodyguards

Commander of the legion

What You'll Need

Your weapons and armor could save your life in battle, so get the best you can. The army will provide some of this equipment for legionaries, but if you are an auxiliary, you must pay for your own clothes and weapons. If you are a cavalryman you must provide and equip your own horses. You can choose your battle armor—as long as you have the approval of your commanding officer.

Ceremonial armor

▼ For cavalry displays or festival parades, officers and their men wear beautiful ceremonial armor. They stage cavalry charges and mock battles, using weapons with wooden tips instead of iron.

We soldiers like to fight hard and play hard, too!

Auxiliary soldiers

Bow

Arrows

Chainmail

Sword

Stabbing sword

▲ Auxiliary soldiers are recruited from different lands. This archer is from the Middle East. Auxiliaries use their own weapons and armor.

A soldier's shield

▲ Your shield (*scutum*) is made from wooden strips glued together and covered with leather or felt. It should be about a yard (1 m) high to cover the most vulnerable parts of your body.

Horse armor

▼ For cavalry displays horses wear bronze eye shields and metal or leather masks as armor. Sometimes they have metal decorations on their bridles, reins, and saddle straps.

Hardy helmets

The best helmets are made of iron with leather or wool padding. They have cheek covers and a rigid neck-guard at the back.

The look of a legionary soldier

▼ This is how you'll look as a legionary soldier, fully dressed and ready for battle.

Galea (helmet to protect the head, face, and neck)

Gladius (short sword worn on the right)

Lorica segmentata (metal body armor held together by leather straps)

Woolen tunic worn under the armor

Caligae (strong sandals with iron hobnails in the sole)

Pilum (javelin)

Pugio (dagger)

Protective apron of metal discs

Packed and ready

You will carry your supplies on a wooden pole over your shoulder. Take food, a water bottle, a cooking pot, and tools—a spade, a scythe, a mattock, and an ax. Wear warm clothes under your tunic. Also try short pants or loose calf-length trousers and woolen socks.

Army Discipline

Once you're sworn into the army you must behave like a soldier. Obey orders without any hesitation or question. Good discipline in battle is very important. Lives may be at risk if you disobey orders. Don't argue with officers, or the centurion will punish you and all the others in your tent-group, too. The army will keep you very busy and very tired, so you won't have the energy to get into trouble! You'll be marching, battle training, and doing "fatigues" (all the dirty jobs).

Swearing an oath

▶ New recruits swear a solemn oath that binds them for 25 years or until they die in battle. You must honor the emperor, obey your officers, and never desert the army.

Gold coins

Officers in charge

Officers (centurions) are in charge of army discipline. They are tough, brave soldiers who began their careers like you.

I will serve my emperor. My word is my bond.

Viaticum

◀ Don't lose these three gold coins! That would get your army career off to a very bad start. They are called a *viaticum* and will be given to you after you have been sworn in, to pay for your journey to the training camp.

Rise and shine

Centurion

▶ Every morning at daybreak you must report to the centurion in charge. He will give orders for jobs to be done today.

Fatigues

▼ As a junior soldier, you'll do all the dirty jobs like cleaning the lavatories, clearing blocked drains, or stoking the bathhouse fires. You might join the other soldiers outside the camp felling timber, quarrying stone, and building roads. Fatigues will harden your body and make you a stronger fighter but will leave you exhausted at the end of every day.

Soldier doing fatigues

Punishments

▼ Soldiers who rebel or run away will be beaten to death by their comrades. If a whole century (group of 80 men) disobeys orders, it might be decimated (though this was very rare), which means one in every ten men will be killed.

Soldiers punishing a rebel

Things to do

Daily rota

▶ If you oversleep, check the duty rota. You will find your name there with the tasks you have to do beside it.

Learning New Skills

By the end of your first year you'll be a skilled fighter. But you won't start weapons training until you've completed an intensive marching course. This will give you strength and stamina and teach you to act as part of a team. If you fail, you'll be sent home in disgrace or put on punishment rations of bread until you succeed. You must do lots of exercise—running, jumping, and swimming— to prepare for war. If you are smart, you may learn skills like first aid or planning and building new forts. The army can offer you a rewarding career if you're prepared to work hard.

Cooking

▶ Cooking skills come in handy when you are away from the fort. Learn to make soup from lentils or grains and how to soak *buccellata* (dry biscuits) in water to make porridge.

We've been marching all day long in this wretched rain.

Marching all day long

The first four months of training are devoted to marching. You'll learn to march in step with your comrades on the parade ground. Then you'll go on route marches, in uniform at first, then carrying all your kit. ▲

By the end of training you'll have to cover 22 miles (36 km) in five hours or face a beating from the centurion. The Roman army must move faster than its enemies or face defeat.

Expert soldiers

▼ The army needs many different specialists, like architects, surveyors, and engineers. If you do well as an ordinary soldier, you might train as an *immunis*—an expert who is let off routine duties to perform important tasks.

Expert soldiers working as surveyors

Skilled soldiers

▼ You might be chosen to train for a craft or trade. Carpenters, stonemasons, and bricklayers are kept busy building forts. If you qualify you'll do this work, and ordinary soldiers will do the laboring jobs for you.

Defense formations

▶ You will learn defensive formations like the *testudo* (tortoise). You link shields to form an impenetrable "shell" above your heads.

Soldiers in the tortoise formation

Fight school

▶ At daily weapons training, you'll learn how to fight by attacking hefty wooden posts about six feet (1.8 m) high. At first you'll use wooden swords and wicker shields. Once you have learned the basics, you'll train with real weapons.

Where Will You Live?

Soldiers have to live in many places—some cozy and comfortable, others damp and cold, perhaps even dangerous! The army has two types of living quarters. Marching camps are usually temporary tent-cities, built to house legions as they travel or when staying at important building sites. Forts are the permanent headquarters for legions living far from Rome. They have barracks, kitchens, lavatories, stables, stores and sometimes even baths and temples. There is also a house for the commander.

Army camp

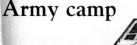

Rows of tents

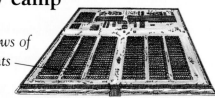

▲ A camp is like a small town. Tents are always in the same rows, so everyone can pitch his tent in a hurry and find his way back, even in the dark. If there are enemies nearby, you'll defend the camp by digging ditches and ramparts (earthen walls).

Barracks

▼ Your barracks room is crowded. The eight men in your *contubernium* (tent-group) share a space no bigger than four yards (3.6 m) square. Your centurion has his own, larger room at one end of the barracks block.

Wouldn't it be nice to have a room each?

Tents

On campaign, you'll live in a *papilio* (tent) made of goatskin. It is strong and waterproof, but it can be smelly. Use wooden tent pegs to secure it. Cover the ground with straw, heather, or dry grass.

Beds

▼ Bunk beds are hard and narrow with rough woolen blankets and straw mattresses. Your weapons, armor, and gear are kept in a little storeroom next door.

The sooner we are centurions, the better.

Fort lookouts

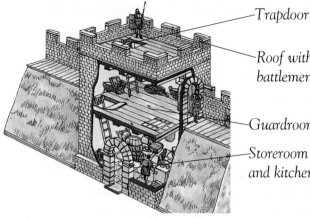

Trapdoor

Roof with battlements

Guardroom

Storeroom and kitchen

▲ Lookouts keep watch from towers built into the fort walls. Every tower has rooms where off-duty men eat and rest.

▶ Each fort is surrounded by a ditch, bank, and walls. All visitors must report to the sentries at the gates.

Watchtower

Praetorium (commander's house)

Gate

Barracks where soldiers sleep

Home sweet home?

▶ Each barracks block houses a century (80 soldiers) and a centurion. Barracks are built of local timber, stone, or lath and plaster and are heated by small stoves in every sleeping room.

15

How Much Will You Earn?

The army pays quite well. Legionary soldiers (*milites*) earn about 300 *denarii* each year—almost twice a teacher's salary. But the army will keep a lot of it to pay for food, clothes, weapons, and lodging. You'll have to save some too—don't waste it on gambling or wine! If you get promoted, you will earn much more. Junior officers earn one-and-a-half times normal pay and senior officers earn double. Top centurions receive up to 15 times more than the men they command.

Keeping records

▼ The commander of the fort has a staff of army clerks who keep records of soldiers' pay and all the fort's expenses.

Stylus (pen)

Tabula cera (wax tablet)

Army scribe

Secret store

▼ The best place to keep all your savings is in a strongbox in the secret storeroom under the legion's shrine. The statues of the emperor and gods of war will guard it.

The gods will protect your savings, soldier.

The cost of living

An ordinary soldier can't afford many luxuries. If you become a *principalis* (junior officer) or a centurion, you'll have much more money to spend. Look at the list (*right*) for some idea of the price of goods.

A purse to protect

▼ Keep money safe in a metal purse like this. It has to be taken off your wrist before you can open it.

Roman currency

▼ These Roman coins are used all over the empire, wherever the army sends you.

2 dupondii = 1 sestertius
4 sestertii = 1 denarius
25 sestertii = 1 aureus

One dupondius can buy two donkeys, but one aureus can buy 100!

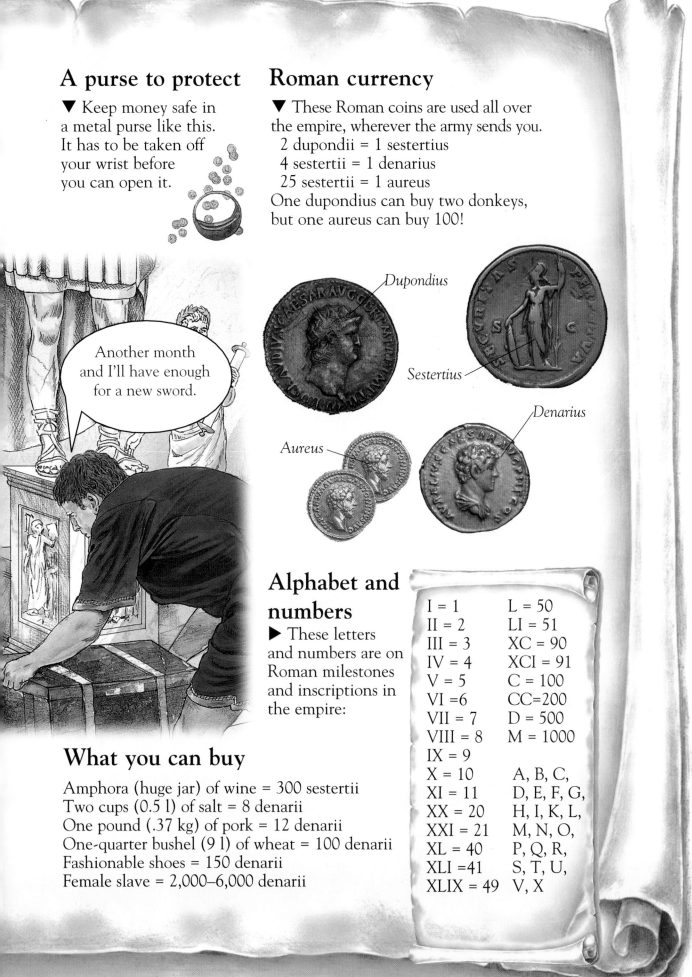

Another month and I'll have enough for a new sword.

Dupondius

Sestertius

Aureus

Denarius

Alphabet and numbers

▶ These letters and numbers are on Roman milestones and inscriptions in the empire:

I = 1	L = 50
II = 2	LI = 51
III = 3	XC = 90
IV = 4	XCI = 91
V = 5	C = 100
VI = 6	CC = 200
VII = 7	D = 500
VIII = 8	M = 1000
IX = 9	
X = 10	A, B, C,
XI = 11	D, E, F, G,
XX = 20	H, I, K, L,
XXI = 21	M, N, O,
XL = 40	P, Q, R,
XLI = 41	S, T, U,
XLIX = 49	V, X

What you can buy

Amphora (huge jar) of wine = 300 sestertii
Two cups (0.5 l) of salt = 8 denarii
One pound (.37 kg) of pork = 12 denarii
One-quarter bushel (9 l) of wheat = 100 denarii
Fashionable shoes = 150 denarii
Female slave = 2,000–6,000 denarii

Join the Army, See the World

There are always troops guarding the frontiers of the Roman Empire, so prepare to spend years far from home. Think of your time abroad as an "adventure," but it won't be a vacation. The frontier lands are wild, lawless places where you will fight local tribes who want to drive the Romans out. You'll see some spectacular scenery, but you'll realize that few places have such good weather as Italy.

A Roman warship

▼ A typical Roman warship is 148 feet (45 m) long and 30 feet (9 m) wide. It carries 600 soldiers, and is crewed by 250 sailors and slaves.

Outposts of the empire

▼ You may be sent to guard Hadrian's Wall, on the border of England and Scotland. It stretches 75 miles (120 km) across windy moorland where there is usually snow in winter.

This ballista (big crossbow) fires metal bolts

Soldiers ready to defend the ship

Transport

▼The army has priority on Roman roads. Travelers give way to troops and their wagons.

Farm cart

This place is freezing! I wish I were back in Rome.

Roads and bridges

Top layer of shaped stone slabs

Layer of stone chippings, pebbles, or gravel

Layer of stone blocks

Base layer of smooth sand or soil

▲ If you're sent to put down a rebellion on a distant frontier, you'll almost certainly march along a well-made Roman road. These roads are engineering masterpieces, carefully planned and surveyed to take the straightest course between important towns.

Wooden towers on deck allow soldiers to keep a lookout for enemy ships and shelter soldiers from attack

The warship is powered by men rowing

Senior officers

Rest and Recreation

Regular duties keep you busy for most of the day, but the army does give you time off. Explore the surroundings of your fort or camp. Most forts are near a *vicus* (civilian village) with many shops, stalls, and taverns. Villagers are friendly—they make a good living from their Roman customers. Many lonely Roman soldiers fall in love with local girls. The army also holds chariot races and gladiator fights on festival days.

Theater

▶ If your fort is close to a town, you might see a play at the local theater.

Roman actor

Come and get some food. You must be hungry after all that marching.

Relaxing at the baths

▼ After a long march, refresh yourself with an afternoon at the baths. Most forts have a bathhouse, with steamrooms, cold plunge pools, and deep, warm communal baths.

A day at the races

▼ For an exciting day out, join the huge crowds watching chariot races in the amphitheater.

Chariot race

Family life

Regular soldiers are not allowed to marry while in the service, because they are away for months on end. But "unofficial" marriages with local women are overlooked.

Knucklebones and dice

Dice

Knucklebones

▶ Gambling is very popular. Will you bet on catching knucklebones or on the fall of the dice? Always check dice very carefully before you start to play. They are often "loaded" (unfairly weighted) to allow cheats to win.

The gladiators

▼ In the arena of the crowded amphitheater, highly paid gladiators (professional fighters), dressed in splendid armor, battle against one another or against wild beasts from the countryside.

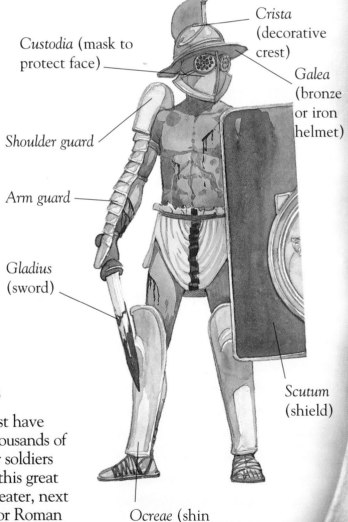

Custodia (mask to protect face)

Crista (decorative crest)

Galea (bronze or iron helmet)

Shoulder guard

Arm guard

Gladius (sword)

Scutum (shield)

Ocreae (shin guards to protect your lower legs)

Roman amphitheaters

◀ It must have taken thousands of hours for soldiers to build this great amphitheater, next to a major Roman fort.

Seats   *Arena*

Dangers of the Job

Army life is dangerous. Many soldiers die from battle injuries or accidents on army building sites. But soldiers are stronger and better trained to face risks than most other men. The army feeds its men well with meat and vegetables almost every day. It provides clean water and good sanitation in forts and camps, too. This means that you will be less likely to die from disease.

Operations

▲ Operations are risky, but Roman soldiers get excellent medical care. Army doctors use alcohol and herbs as anesthetics. They stitch up wounds and keep them clean. They can amputate damaged limbs, and they use antiseptics like turpentine and salt.

The battlefield

▼ Going into battle is the most dangerous thing you'll ever do. Stay calm—remember your training and use your weapons as you were taught.

The enemy has wounded me.

Medical equipment

Army doctors have several ► ways to treat wounds and diseases. They apply ointments and give patients medicine, and have a variety of equipment for examining and healing wounds.

Heavy artillery

The Roman army is proud of its large war machines. But ballistas, onagers (huge catapults), and battering rams can be dangerous, because they require great skill to operate.

forceps

forceps

probe

spatula

spatula

Medical care

Operating table

Preparing medicines

Bandages

Bandaged leg

▶ Hospitals are an essential part of every fort. They are equipped with beds, operating tables, linen for bandages, and stoves for brewing medicines and preparing drinks.

◀ Lead stopper from a jar of "British root" medicine, which was thought to cure scurvy.

Medical officer helping an injured soldier

▶ In battle, you will see medical staff in the thick of the fighting giving first aid   to wounded soldiers.

◀ Soldiers who have survived a battle injury often hang offerings of thanks in the temple at their fort. They are shaped like their wounded limbs.

Leg-shaped offering

Ear-shaped offering

Are You Officer Material?

Smart and hard-working soldiers can have a successful army career. There are two ways to become an officer—by promotion from the ranks of ordinary soldiers or by noble birth. If you come from an ordinary Roman family, you'll first train to be an *immunis*, an expert in one special skill. Next you may be a *tesserarius* (commander of a guard troop) and then a *signifer* (standard-bearer). If you show promise, senior officers will appoint you *optio* (deputy centurion). You will then train until you achieve centurion grade.

Staff meetings

▼ Every morning there is a meeting of centurions at the commander's quarters.

Good morning, centurions.

The path of a brilliant career

Top officers are chosen from proud, noble families.

First they will become senators and discuss government policy.

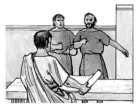
Then they serve as magistrates in a distant province.

They might also be elected as representatives of the people.

▼ At their morning meetings, centurions report on the men in their units, the day's duties, and any problems in the fort or camp. They plan any special tasks and order fresh supplies. They also choose a new secret *tessera* (password) for that day to prevent enemies from entering the camp or fort.

Let us begin. Today's password will be "vitis."

Legionary centurion

▼ Centurions are the backbone of the Roman army. They are strict and can be harsh and ruthless, but everyone admires them for their bravery and fighting skills.

Galea (iron or bronze helmet)

Vitis (vine wood cane, a sign of rank)

Phalera (medallion with a monster's head to drive away harm)

Lorica (metal breastplate)

Cingulum (belt)

Pugio (dagger)

Gladius (sword)

Bracae (knee breeches)

Caligae (tough sandals)

Next they will join the army as *tribunes* (staff officers).

Then they are promoted to the rank of second-in-command.

Only the best become *legatus*—commander of a legion.

A *legatus* might be made governor of a province.

Could You Land the Top Job?

No—the Roman emperor is head of both the empire and the army. Soldiers honor him in daily prayers. His picture is on the standard they carry into battle to show that they are fighting for him and for all of Rome. Some emperors are excellent soldiers—Trajan won great glory and riches for Rome. He conquered Dacia (Romania), Armenia, and Mesopotamia (Iraq). Others, like Caligula and Nero, were hopeless soldiers and spent no time in the army at all.

Emperor Hadrian

▼ The present emperor, Hadrian, came to power in A.D. 117. He has followed Trajan's example and is a fine army commander. He is eager to establish and defend the Roman Empire's frontiers once and for all.

Victory brings honor

▼ Successful leaders are honored with a "triumph." This is a ceremonial procession through the streets of Rome to receive praise and thanks from the citizens.

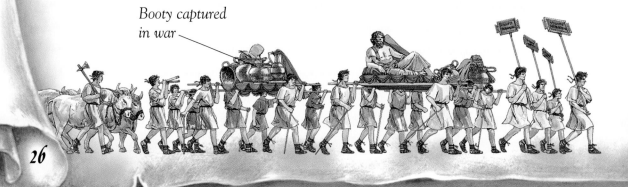

Booty captured in war

Hadrian's Wall

Hadrian often visited the frontier to inspect and encourage his troops. He went to northern Britain and built a vast fortification there called Hadrian's Wall (*see page 18*).

Monuments

◀ In Rome, look out for splendid triumphal arches like this. They are built to honor victorious commanders and their brave soldiers.

> Rome will be proud of what my men have achieved.

Trajan's tower

▼ In A.D. 106, Emperor Trajan decided to build a great monument to celebrate his victories in war. It is a stone pillar about 100 feet (30 m) high. It is decorated with carvings of Trajan and his courageous soldiers.

Emperor Trajan commanding his troops

Captured enemies held hostage

Triumphator (person being honored)

Long-term Prospects

If you survive in the army for 25 years you can expect an honorable retirement. Some soldiers return to the land where they were born; others stay where they last served to live with their unofficial wives and children. Most receive a retirement gift of land, which they can farm for a living. Others might buy a shop or make use of the skills they learned in the army. Soldiers believe their spirit lives on in heaven and gains strength whenever their comrades remember them.

Mithras sacrificing a bull

The army has served us well, sir.

Diploma award

▼ When you retire, your commanding officer will give you a diploma recording your pension rights. Legionary soldiers normally receive ten years' pay. This will be enough to set yourself up in business or to buy a small plot of land.

Diplomas are often made of bronze, so that they will last for the rest of a soldier's life. Guard your diploma well —it is your passport to many years of comfortable retirement.

Bronze pension diploma

A soldier's faith

◀ Many soldiers worship Mithras—a Middle Eastern god usually shown sacrificing a bull. Mithraism inspires comradeship among soldiers.

Congratulations for many years of good service.

Tombstone tribute

If you die in active service, your family or friends will pay for a tombstone. Your name and details of your army career will be carved on it.

Farming

▲ Many soldiers dream of buying a plot of land. But farming is hard work all year round. In warmer countries you can grow vines and must prune them.

▲ If you decide to rear livestock, you need to give them fresh straw for bedding and fresh hay to eat every day. They will also need daily water supplies.

▲ In summer you'll need extra help with the harvest. The corn needs to be cut, dried, and then carted away to be stored safely before it is threshed.

▲ Raising sheep may be easier, but you'll be kept busy with the lambing in spring. You will also have to shear their wool in summer.

Your Interview

Answer these questions to test your knowledge, then look at page 32 to find out if you have what it takes to get the job.

Q1 How will you spend your first months in the army?
A learning to build roads
B learning to march
C learning to fight

Q2 As an ordinary soldier, how much will you earn?
A 500 denarii per year
B 100 denarii per year
C 300 denarii per year

Q3 Where might you travel to on duty?
A America
B England
C China

Q4 Whom will you obey at all times?
A army officers
B your father
C the gods

Q5 Who will look after you if you are injured?
A your comrades
B army doctors
C slave women

Q6 How will you learn to fight?
A by attacking prisoners
B by attacking new recruits
C by attacking wooden posts

Q7 Where will you live when in the army?
A in tents or barracks
B in wooden huts
C in Roman towns

Q8 How many years will you have to serve?
A 15 years
B 25 years
C 35 years

Glossary

Amphitheater. Small circular arena for performances.

Amputate. To cut off all or part of a limb.

Anesthetic. Drug that puts people to sleep for operations.

Antiseptic. Substance that kills germs.

Armorers. Craftsmen who make weapons and armor.

Artillery. Weapons that shoot bullets, arrows, or metal bolts.

Auxiliaries. Soldiers recruited from lands not in the Roman Empire.

Ballista. A large crossbow operated by several people.

Cavalry. Soldiers on horseback.

Chain mail. Armor made from linked metal rings.

Citizens. People born in the Roman Empire.

Communal. Shared by people.

Fortification. A wall that strengthens a building or place.

Lath. A thin strip of wood.

Legion. Basic Roman army unit of about 4,800 soldiers.

Mattock. Heavy spade.

Mithraism. Worship of the god Mithras.

Onager. A type of large catapult for destroying fortifications.

Rampart. Wall of pounded earth.

Sanitation. Drains, lavatories, and other means by which living areas are kept clean.

Scurvy. Disease caused by lack of fresh fruit and vitamin C.

Scythe. Tool for cutting long grass.

Standard. Flag or symbol of a nation.

Surveyor. Someone who measures land.

Tribute. Payment that must be made or is given to show respect for someone.

Turpentine. Sticky gum from plants, used as an anesthetic.

Viaticum. Money used for travel expenses.

Index

Have You Got the Job?

Count up your correct answers (*below right*) and find out if you got the job.

Your score:

8 Congratulations, you're a born soldier.

7 A little more effort would get you the job.

5–6 Showed promise at the interview—we'll remember your name.

3–4 Not quite ready for the army yet. Try again later.

Fewer than 3 You must try harder if you want to be a Roman soldier.

1 (B) page 12
2 (C) page 16
3 (B) page 18
4 (A) pages 10, 28
5 (B) pages 22–23
6 (C) page 13
7 (A) pages 14–15
8 (B) pages 10–11